Law Enforcement

Motorcycle Police

by Michael Green

Consultant:
Sergeant Richard Elias
Mountainview Police Department
Mountainview, California

RiverFront Books
an imprint of Franklin Watts
A Division of Grolier Publishing
New York   London   Hong Kong   Sydney
Danbury, Connecticut

RiverFront Books
http://publishing.grolier.com
Copyright © 1999 Capstone Press. All rights reserved.
No part of this book may be reproduced without written permission from the publisher.
The publisher takes no responsibility for the use of any of the materials or methods
described in this book, nor for the products thereof.
Printed in the United States of America.
Published simultaneously in Canada.

Library of Congress Cataloging-in-Publication Data
Green, Michael, 1952-
    Motorcycle police/by Michael Green.
    p. cm.—(Law enforcement)
    Includes bibliographical references and index.
    Summary: An introduction to the law enforcement officers known as
motorcycle police, including their history, functions, responsibilities, training,
equipment, and the criminals they target.
    ISBN 0-7368-0187-1
    1. Motorcycle police—Juvenile literature. [1. Motorcycle police.
2. Occupations.] I. Title. II. Series: Green, Michael, 1952- Law enforcement.
HV8020.G74 1999
363.2'32—dc21
                                                          98-31540
                                                              CIP
                                                               AC

Editorial Credits

Connie R. Colwell, editor; Timothy Halldin, cover designer; Kimberly Danger
    and Sheri Gosewisch, photo researchers

Photo Credits

Barbara J. Coxe, 16
California Highway Patrol Museum, 6, 11, 12, 24, 26, 28
Kate Boykin, 8, 36
Leslie O'Shaughnessy, cover, 14, 21, 22, 34
Mark C. Ide, 4, 30
Michael Green, 19, 32, 38, 42-43
Photo Network/McDonald Photography, 41

Table of Contents

Chapter 1 Motorcycle Police 5

Chapter 2 History of Motorcycle Police.......... 9

Chapter 3 Motorcycle Police Officers............ 15

Chapter 4 Training 23

Chapter 5 Police Motorcycles 29

Chapter 6 Equipment and Safety 35

Features

Photo Diagram 42

Words to Know 44

To Learn More 45

Useful Addresses 46

Internet Sites 47

Index 48

Motorcycle Police

Motorcycle police officers are police officers who patrol on motorcycles. These officers are like other patrol officers. They keep streets and highways safe. But motorcycle police officers patrol on motorcycles instead of on foot, on bicycles, or in cars.

Patrolling with Motorcycles

Motorcycles are good for patrolling small or crowded areas. Motorcycles are smaller than police cars. This means that officers on motorcycles can ride through or around traffic jams. These officers also can patrol alleys that are too narrow for cars.

Motorcycle police officers patrol on motorcycles.

Motorcycles can tip over easily.

Motorcycles are a quick way to patrol. Officers on motorcycles can travel faster than officers on foot or bicycles. Officers on motorcycles sometimes arrive at crime scenes faster than other patrol officers. They also can patrol large areas in short amounts of time.

Problems with Motorcycles

Police officers can have problems patrolling on motorcycles. Motorcycles cannot carry as much as police cars. Officers on motorcycles need help to bring people to police departments.

Motorcycles are not useful in bad weather. Motorcycles are difficult to operate safely in rain or snow. Police cars have roofs to cover riders in bad weather. Motorcycles do not have roofs to protect their riders from bad weather.

Motorcycles can be difficult to control. This is true especially on wet or slippery roads. Motorcycles only have two wheels. They can tip over easily. Ice, snow, and rain make it more difficult to control motorcycles. Many police departments do not use motorcycles during the winter months.

Chapter 2

History of Motorcycle Police

In the 1800s, police officers patrolled on foot or on horseback. But officers on foot could not move very fast or travel far. They could only patrol small areas. Officers on horseback could patrol larger areas. But their horses needed to stop for food and water. The horses sometimes got sick or hurt.

Some police departments began using bicycles to patrol during the 1890s. Officers on bicycles could go faster and farther than officers on foot. Bicycles also did not need food or water.

Some officers still patrol on foot or horseback today.

Traffic Problems

In the early 1900s, many people in the United States and Canada began to travel in cars. For example, the population of the city of New York was more than 1.5 million. Many of these people drove cars on the city's streets. The streets became crowded with cars.

Few states or provinces had traffic laws. People often drove their cars too fast. Sometimes people were hurt or killed in traffic accidents. Officers on bicycles could not travel as fast as people in cars. Police departments needed a way to catch speeders.

A Solution

In the late 1800s, some inventors attached motors to their bicycles. The motors moved the bicycles along more quickly than pedaling. People called these vehicles motorcycles. By 1903, businesses sold motorcycles to the public.

In 1911, the New York Police Department (NYPD) formed a motorcycle patrol unit. The NYPD motorcycle unit tried to control the

Early motorcycle patrol units had difficulty patrolling on unpaved roads.

traffic on New York's busy city streets. Officers on motorcycles could travel as fast as people in speeding cars.

But the early motorcycle officers faced some problems. They needed to drive their motorcycles on smooth, paved roads. In the early 1900s, many roads in the United States and Canada were not paved. Most roads were

rough and bumpy. Motorcycle police officers could not patrol easily on these roads. Most police departments did not use motorcycle units until the 1920s.

After World War I (1914-1918), cities started to fix their roads. More roads were paved. More and more people traveled by car. This caused more traffic and more accidents. In 1924, more than 19,000 people died in car accidents. Many police departments formed motorcycle patrol units to help solve traffic problems. The motorcycle police officers worked to keep roads safe for people in the United States and Canada.

Many police departments formed motorcycle patrol units to help solve traffic problems.

Chapter 3

Motorcycle Police Officers

Most police departments are divided into groups called divisions and units. The patrol division is the largest group of officers in most police departments. Smaller groups of officers serve in units.

Most motorcycle police officers work in the traffic unit. The traffic unit is one part of the patrol division. Officers in the traffic unit enforce traffic laws by trying to catch people who break these laws. They handle traffic accidents. They also support car patrol officers.

Officers in the traffic division try to catch people who break traffic laws.

At one time, motorcycle police officers paced vehicles to see if the drivers were speeding.

Traffic Laws

The main duty of motorcycle police officers is to enforce traffic laws. Officers give tickets to some people who break traffic laws. These papers tell people a police officer saw them break a traffic law. Some people who receive tickets must pay fines or go to court. Others must attend traffic school classes to learn about traffic laws.

Some traffic laws are more serious than others. For example, drinking too much alcohol before driving is one serious traffic law violation. Motorcycle police officers arrest people who drink too much alcohol and drive.

Speeding

Motorcycle police officers try to stop people from speeding. Speeding is another traffic law violation. It is against the law to drive vehicles faster than the speed limit.

Motorcycle police officers once followed cars closely to see if the drivers were speeding. This was called pacing. Pacing was dangerous and not effective for the officers. Officers often had to drive very fast to pace speeding cars. These officers sometimes had accidents. Also, some speeders slowed down because they saw the officers. This made it difficult to catch speeders.

In the 1970s, many officers started using radar guns to catch speeders. These machines fit in the officers' hands. The guns sent out radio beams. The beams bounced off the passing vehicles and back to the radar guns. The radar guns then showed the speed of the vehicles.

To catch speeders, officers parked their motorcycles in safe or hidden locations. They then stood in places where speeding drivers could not see them. Some officers stood under bridges. Others stood behind turns in the road or at the tops of hills. The officers then pointed the radar guns at passing vehicles.

In the 1980s, some drivers began buying radar detectors for their cars. Radar detectors beep when they sense nearby radar beams. Speeders slow their cars when they hear the beeps. Radar detectors can make it difficult for officers to catch speeders.

In the 1990s, some motorcycle police officers began using laser guns. Laser guns work like radar guns. But laser guns send out beams of unseen light instead of radio beams. Vehicles pass through the light beams. The laser guns then show officers the speeds of passing

Some motorcycle police officers use laser guns to learn the speed of passing vehicles.

vehicles. Radar detectors cannot sense these laser guns.

Today, some motorcycle police officers are taught to judge the speeds of vehicles by eyesight. These officers also measure speeds with radar or laser guns. This helps officers prove that drivers are actually speeding.

Traffic Accidents

Motorcycle police officers sometimes help at traffic accidents. The officers make sure that injured people receive medical care. They also direct traffic around accident scenes.

Officers investigate traffic accidents. They talk to the people involved in accidents. They also talk to people who see accidents.

Officers try to figure out the causes of accidents. Sometimes people cause accidents. Some people cause accidents when they are tired or not paying attention. Other people cause accidents by breaking traffic laws. Officers may give tickets to people responsible for accidents. Officers sometimes arrest these people.

Motorcycle police officers sometimes investigate traffic accidents.

Officers write reports when they are done with investigations. They write the details of accidents in these reports. The traffic division uses these reports to improve traffic safety. The traffic division sometimes assigns more motorcycle police officers to an area with many accidents. These reports also can be used in court to help judges decide the causes of accidents.

Chapter 4

Training

Police officers need training and experience to become motorcycle police officers. They must know how to ride police motorcycles. They must learn how to care for their motorcycles. The officers also must learn how to stay safe while they patrol on motorcycles.

Police Motorcycles

Police motorcycles are different than regular motorcycles. Police motorcycles carry more equipment than most regular motorcycles. This extra equipment changes the balance of police motorcycles. Police motorcycles sometimes travel faster than most regular motorcycles. This extra speed makes them harder to control.

Officers need to learn how to ride police motorcycles before they can become motorcycle police officers.

It takes a great deal of special training to operate police motorcycles safely. Officers who want to be motorcycle police officers first must work as car patrol officers. They then can apply for the job of motorcycle police officer. These officers must take a variety of classes. They train both in classrooms and on the road. Officers who pass these classes become motorcycle police officers.

CHP Motorcycle Training

Until the 1950s, most motorcycle police officers were not trained for their special jobs. They did not learn about the differences between police motorcycles and regular motorcycles. The officers did not always know how to drive their motorcycles safely. Many had serious accidents.

In 1968, the California Highway Patrol (CHP) created a training program for motorcycle police officers. The program is held at the CHP Academy in Sacramento, California. The officers in the CHP program

Today, many motorcycle police officers train on test tracks.

Officers practice riding motorcycles on the CHP Academy's test track.

receive 82 hours of training. The program lasts two weeks.

The officers learn many things at the CHP Academy. The officers learn the names of motorcycle parts. They learn what each part does. They learn how to fix their motorcycles. The officers learn how to maintain their motorcycles to keep them in good shape.

Officers at the CHP Academy also learn how to ride their motorcycles. They practice riding motorcycles on the CHP Academy's test track. Academy teachers set up plastic cones on the track. The officers try to ride between the cones without knocking them over. This helps officers learn to ride in narrow spaces. The officers then ride on streets and highways with CHP Academy teachers.

Today, many large police departments have motorcycle training schools. But some small police departments do not have their own training schools. They must send their officers to the schools run by larger police departments. Many of the small police departments send their officers to the CHP Academy.

Chapter 5

Police Motorcycles

Police motorcycles built before 1930 were simple. Some were only bicycles with motors attached to them. In the 1930s, manufacturers started making new types of motorcycles. These motorcycles were better suited for police work.

Early Police Motorcycles

Three North American companies built the first police motorcycles. The Harley-Davidson Motor Company is the oldest motorcycle manufacturer in the world. Harley-Davidson built many of the first police motorcycles. The Excelsior-Henderson and Indian Motorcycle Companies also built early police motorcycles.

Motorcycles built before 1930 were simple.

Today, many police departments use Harley-Davidson police motorcycles to patrol.

Police departments bought police motorcycles from the three North American motorcycle companies for many years. But the Excelsior-Henderson Motorcycle Company went out of business in 1931. The Indian Motorcycle Company closed in 1953. In the early 1970s, Japanese and Italian motorcycle companies began to sell police motorcycles in the United States.

Harley-Davidson Police Motorcycles

Today, Harley-Davidson motorcycles are still the most popular police motorcycles in the United States. More than 900 U.S. police departments use these motorcycles.

Harley-Davidson has made police motorcycles since 1909. Harley-Davidson makes different kinds of police motorcycles. These kinds of motorcycles are called models. The FLHP Road King is one Harley-Davidson model. The Road King weighs 712 pounds (323 kilograms). Many U.S. police departments use the Road King to patrol.

The Electra Glide is another Harley-Davidson model. It is similar to the Road King. But it has more features. For example, the Electra Glide has a special cover on its handlebars to protect officers' hands. Many police departments use the Electra Glide to patrol today.

Some police departments use Kawasaki police motorcycles to patrol.

Kawasaki Police Motorcycles

Some police departments use police motorcycles made by Kawasaki. This Japanese company has made motorcycles since the 1940s.

Many police departments use the Kawasaki Police 1000 motorcycle to patrol. This model weighs about 595 pounds (270 kilograms). It has special features such as speakers on the handlebars.

BMW Police Motorcycles

BMW is a German motorcycle company. It has made motorcycles since 1923. BMW police motorcycles are the most popular police motorcycles around the world.

In 1998, the CHP bought 150 BMW police motorcycles. These police motorcycles are called R 1100 RT-P motorcycles. The R 1100 RT-P weighs about 622 pounds (282 kilograms). These motorcycles have special brakes that help officers stop quickly. They also have heated handlebars to keep officers' hands warm in cold weather.

Today, many police departments in North America are testing BMW police motorcycles. They want to compare BMW police motorcycles to other police motorcycles. They want to see which motorcycles are best for patrolling. BMW is the only company that makes the special brakes for police motorcycles. Some BMW police motorcycles also are less expensive than other companies' models.

Chapter 6

Equipment and Safety

Motorcycle police officers have special equipment on their motorcycles. This gear helps the officers enforce traffic laws. The equipment also keeps officers safe.

Radios

Early police motorcycle radios were only receivers. Motorcycle police officers could receive radio messages from police headquarters on the radios. But the officers could not send radio messages back to police headquarters. The officers had to stop and use a telephone to reply to their messages.

Motorcycle police officers have radios to help them send and receive messages.

Police motorcycle officers' helmets have a small speaker and a microphone attached to them.

Police motorcycles began using two-way radios in the 1940s. Two-way radios can send and receive messages. Today, motorcycle police officers do not need telephones to talk with police departments.

Today, many police motorcycles have two radios. One radio is large. It attaches to the motorcycle. This radio works well over long and short distances. The second radio is smaller. This small hand-held radio attaches to the officer's belt. It is powered by a small battery. This radio works well for short distances. Officers use the small radio when they are away from their motorcycles.

Speakers and Microphones

Today, many motorcycle police officers also have a small speaker and a microphone inside their helmets. The speaker lets officers hear messages from police headquarters. The officers speak into the microphone. This sends messages back to police departments and to other officers.

Most motorcycle police officers also have a speaker and microphone attached to the front of their motorcycles. Officers use these to send and receive messages when they are not wearing their helmets.

Other Equipment

Motorcycle police officers use other equipment to help them enforce traffic laws. Some of this

Most police motorcycles have saddlebags to carry equipment.

equipment also helps them protect citizens.

Many officers carry first-aid kits and fire extinguishers on their motorcycles. These items help officers take care of injured motorists.

Most police motorcycles have saddlebags on the backs of their motorcycles. These storage cases can hold officers' ticket books, maps, gloves, and other equipment.

Safety Clothing

Most motorcycle police officers wear special bullet-proof vests under their shirts. These vests protect officers' chests and backs from bullets.

Some officers wear leather jackets and leather boots. This tough material made from animal skin protects the officers from cold weather and wind. Leather also protects officers' skin if they fall off their motorcycles.

All officers wear helmets. Helmets protect officers' heads during falls and traffic accidents.

Many officers also wear special glasses to protect their eyes. These glasses do not break if objects hit them.

Safety Equipment

Police motorcycles have special features to protect officers. Motorcycle police officers sometimes closely follow cars or trucks on the road. These vehicles sometimes kick up rocks and trash behind their wheels. Officers can be hurt by these objects. Police motorcycles have windshields to protect officers from objects. These strong pieces of plastic or glass are attached to the front of motorcycles.

Police motorcycles have safety guards. These strong metal bars extend from both sides of the motorcycle's engine. The bars keep the motorcycles from falling on top of the officers during accidents.

Some police motorcycles also have fairings in front of their handlebars. These strong pieces of plastic protect officers' hands from weather.

Weapons and Handcuffs

Motorcycle police officers carry weapons to help them protect people and themselves. Most officers carry handguns and bullets. Officers carry their guns in holsters. These cases hold guns until the officers need to use them.

Most motorcycle police officers also carry handcuffs. These metal rings are joined by a chain. Handcuffs lock around prisoners' wrists to keep prisoners from getting away from the

Most police motorcycles have a windshield to protect the officers from injury.

officers. Handcuffs prevent prisoners from hurting themselves or other people.

Officers only use their weapons when they need to protect themselves or other people. Weapons and other equipment help motorcycle police officers keep roads and highways safe for everyone.

Motorcycle Police Equipment

Windshield

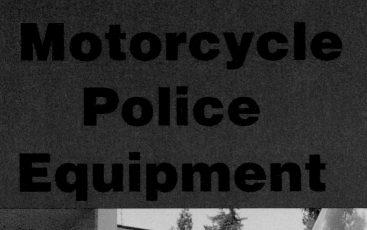

Safety Glasses

Speaker

Hand-held Radio

Saddlebags

Leather Boots

Words to Know

enforce (en-FORSS)—to make sure that a law is obeyed; motorcycle police officers enforce traffic laws by giving tickets and arresting people.

fairings (FAIR-ingz)—plastic guards on a motorcycle's handlebars that protect the rider's hands from weather

fiberglass (FYE-bur-glass)—a strong material made from fine threads of glass

handcuffs (HAND-kuhfs)—metal rings joined by a chain that are locked around a prisoner's wrists to prevent escape

investigate (in-VESS-tuh-gate)—to gather facts in order to discover who committed a crime or who caused an accident

receiver (ri-SEE-vur)—a piece of equipment that receives radio signals and changes them into sounds

violate (VYE-uh-late)—to break a rule or a law

To Learn More

Green, Michael. *Bicycle Patrol Officers*. Law Enforcement. Mankato, Minn.: RiverFront Books, 1999.

Green, Michael. *Military Motorcycles*. Land and Sea. Mankato, Minn.: Capstone Press, 1997.

Jay, Jackson. *Motorcycles*. Rollin'. Mankato, Minn.: Capstone Press, 1996.

Kahaner, Ellen. *Motorcycles*. Cruisin'. Mankato, Minn.: Capstone Press, 1990.

Useful Addresses

**Blue Knights International Law Enforcement
Motorcycle Club, Inc., Ontario Chapter**
P.O. Box 32553
Richmond Hill, ON L4C IAO
Canada

California Highway Patrol
Office of Public Affairs
P.O. Box 942898
Sacramento, CA 94298-0001

**National Motorcycle Museum and Hall
of Fame**
P.O. Box 602
Sturgis, SD 57785

New York City Police Department
Public Affairs Office
One Police Plaza
New York, NY 10038

Internet Sites

Blue Knights International Law Enforcement Motorcycle Club, Inc.
http://www.blueknights.org

BMW Motorcycles
http://www.bmwusacycles.com

California Highway Patrol
http://www.chp.ca.gov

Harley-Davidson Motorcycles
http://www.harley-davidson.com/home.asp

Kawasaki Motorcycles
http://www.kawasaki.com

National Motorcycle Museum and Hall of Fame
http://museum.sturgis-rally.com

Index

bicycles, 5, 6, 9, 10, 29
BMW, 33
bullet-proof vests, 39

California Highway Patrol
  (CHP), 25–27, 33
car patrol, 15, 25

division, 15, 21

Electra Glide, 31
equipment, 23, 35, 37–38,
  39–40, 41
Excelsior-Henderson
  Motorcycle Company, 29
  30

FLHP Road King, 31
foot, 5, 6, 9

Harley-Davidson, 29, 31
helmets, 37, 39
horses, 9

Indian Motorcycle
  Company, 29, 30

Kawasaki, 32

Kawasaki Police 1000, 32

laser guns, 18, 19

microphone, 37
motorcycle patrol, 10, 13, 41

New York City, 10
New York Police
  Department (NYPD), 10

R 1100 RT-P, 33
radar detectors, 18
radar guns, 17, 18, 20
radio, 35-37
road, 7, 11, 13, 18, 25, 39, 41

safety, 21, 39–40
speaker, 32, 37
speeding, 11, 17–18, 20

traffic accidents, 10, 15,
  20–21, 39
traffic law, 10, 15, 16–17,
20, 35, 37

weapons, 40–41